THE
BREXIT
COOKBOOK

VETOED

APPROVED

NIGEL SEWAGE

With Marc Blakewill and James Harris

summersdale

THE BREXIT COOKBOOK

Summersdale Publishers Ltd
46 West Street
Chichester
West Sussex
PO19 1RP
UK

www.summersdale.com

Printed and bound in Croatia

ISBN: 978-1-78685-215-1

Substantial discounts on bulk quantities of Summersdale books are available to corporations, professional associations and other organisations. For details contact general enquiries: telephone: +44 (0) 1243 771107 or email: enquiries@summersdale.com.

For my German wife and my Bulgarian cleaner, my Mozambiquan gardener, my Lebanese PA, my Bangladeshi GP, my Latvian IT support guy, the Brazilian barista at my local cafe, the Nigerian carer who's looking after my aunt, my regular Somali minicab driver, my Irish accountant, my French editor and my Croatian printer. I could've done it much better without you all.

This page is intentionally blank.
(Like the cheque we write to Brussels every year.)

CONTENTS

ABOUT THE AUTHORS

As well as penning books such as *Wanksy: Interpreting a Graffiti Virtuoso* and writing for shows like *Horrible Histories*, *Russell Howard's Good News* and the *4 O'Clock Club*, **Marc Blakewill** and **James Harris** have spent far too long over the years sitting together in cafes. It was in one of these godforsaken places, whilst chewing on a gristly sausage and wondering what on earth was in their scrambled egg, that they conceived *The Brexit Cookbook*: a tome that will surely stop Brexit in its tracks.

It is almost certainly their last cookbook.

Nigel Sewage, meanwhile, is a figment of his own imagination. He doesn't live in Kent.

INTRODUCTION

Congratulations on purchasing *The Brexit Cookbook*. You are now in the vanguard of Britain's fight to retain its culinary independence. For far too long, this country has allowed itself to become swamped with foreign food and it's high time we sent it back to the kitchen with a resounding *'Non!'*

If we're prepared to protect our natural landscape or to save endangered species, why not endangered edibles such as the pork pie, jellied eels or Marmite on toast?

The pretzel-munching, gazpacho-slurping metropolitan elite need to be taught a lesson. We will not sit idly by while our proud national heritage of eating pie and chips, fish and chips, and chips and gravy vanishes before our eyes. Henry V did not win at Agincourt so that we would eat snails. Churchill did not defeat the Nazis so that we would eat sauerkraut. And Thatcher did not swing her handbag in Brussels so that we would eat al dente pasta drizzled in extra virgin olive oil and freshly made pesto sauce.

Yes, it's time to raise the flag and repel the boarders. Who needs Johnny Foreigner when we have the kind of right-thinking, far-sighted heroes who voted to take back control? So whether you care for Welsh rarebit, Scotch eggs, the full English breakfast or whatever they do in Northern Ireland, your country needs you.

Cooking's coming home!

Yours patriotically,

Nigel Sewage

POINTLESS EU REGULATIONS TO BREAK WHILST COOKING: #1

After overcooking a roast, the kitchen will be a total bloody mess, so why not give it a good clean with a 1601 watt vacuum cleaner? Yes, a vacuum cleaner that is one whole unit of energy in excess of the absurd 1600-watt limit the EU has forced on house-proud Britons against their will.

BARNSTORMING BRITISH
BREAKFASTS

Unapologetically
uncontinental offerings

CROISSANT Paltry pastry

INGREDIENTS

- EU-subsidised flour
- EU-subsidised eggs
- EU-subsidised milk
- Apart from that, mostly air

FOREIGNNESS

As foreign as a Parisian waiter with low self-esteem.

SEWAGE SAYS: **FLAKY FLIMFLAM**

Waking up to a French lover in the morning is one thing but waking up to a French breakfast is something else entirely. A shapely body and an air of haughtiness – that's fine in a lover but bloody useless on a plate. You want your morning meal to fortify you, not play hard to get.

THINGS TO WATCH OUT FOR

Cutting the croissant open in order to spread jam on it will result in its immediate disintegration. Just like France in 1940.

FULL ENGLISH Patriotic artery-clogger

INGREDIENTS

- Bacon, eggs, sausages, tomatoes, mushrooms, beans, toast. You know, proper food.
- Grease

PREPARATION

Fry the lot in a greasy pan until saturated in grease. Add grease to taste.

SEWAGE SAYS:
THANK GOD IT'S FRY DAY

APPROVED

This magnificent meal contains all the major food groups: salt, fat and miscellaneous. For years it fuelled the valiant men and women who built the British Empire. As soon as we started eating cornflakes, we lost Rhodesia. So forget your cholesterol levels, say nuts to nutrients and do your patriotic duty. Eat stodge for Britain.

SERVING SUGGESTION

Best appreciated when troubled by the head pounding, dehydration and queasiness of a stonking hangover, i.e. Tuesday to Sunday.

MUESLI You'd be nuts to eat it

INGREDIENTS

- Dust
- Things found down the back of the sofa
- Moisture-sapping dryness

FOREIGNNESS

As foreign as an unclaimed receipt in Brussels.

SEWAGE SAYS: **BIRD FOOD FOR BIRDBRAINS**

You can forgive the Swiss for their opaque banking system, and even their neutrality during the war but, Lord above, you cannot forgive them for the atrocity that is muesli. It's like eating potpourri. There are only two occasions on which you can justifiably serve it as food. First, as a practical joke. Second, if you live on a farm and the pigs are starving.

THINGS TO WATCH OUT FOR

Muesli was apparently created by a Swiss doctor... Note to self: never get ill in Geneva.

PORRIDGE Contains moral fibre

INGREDIENTS

- Rolled oats
- Water or milk
- Hardiness

PREPARATION

Pour water or milk on the oats and bring to the boil. Use a hob, not a microwave – it tastes better when you work for it.

SEWAGE SAYS: GO ON, GET YOUR OATS

The British Citizenship Test runs to several pages and asks questions about things like speed limits, Stonehenge and the length of Holly Willoughby's eyelashes. This tax-payer-funded pub quiz is a complete waste of time and money. If you want to know if someone is genuinely British, you need ask only one question: 'Do you eat porridge?'

SERVING SUGGESTION

Add a small amount of salt or sugar to taste while pointing out obvious left-wing bias on Radio 4's *Today* programme.

CRÊPE Schrödinger's crêpe

INGREDIENTS

- Cardboard left out in the rain
- Butter left out of the fridge

FOREIGNNESS

As foreign as a windscreen wiper on a dodgem car.

SEWAGE SAYS: **A LOAD OF OLD CRÊPE**

It's just a pancake, so why call it anything else? Not only that, but it can come in either sweet or savoury forms. Which is it, for heaven's sake?! This is supposed to be food, not an example of Heisenberg's uncertainty principle.

THINGS TO WATCH OUT FOR

The interior of the crêpe quickly becoming the exterior as the filling falls all over your shirt.

PANCAKE
Properly named pan-made treat

INGREDIENTS

- Ebullient eggs
- Brave butter
- Fearless flour

PREPARATION

Mix in a bowl and pour into a pan while tapping out 'Land of Hope and Glory' with a wooden spoon.

SEWAGE SAYS:
PATRIOTICALLY PANTASTIC

Dostoyevsky said the test of civilisation is how you treat your prisoners. He was right – throw away the key. But the truest test is how you treat your meals. Giving them fancy names is just wrong. In Britain we call a pancake a pancake because it's a bloody pancake. We even eat pancakes on a day called Pancake Day. As transparent as our gloriously unwritten constitution.

SERVING SUGGESTION

Toss in a frying pan while reflecting upon this nation's admirable love of home ownership.

POINTLESS EU REGULATIONS TO BREAK WHILST COOKING: #2

If forced into a situation where you have to prepare a salad, be sure to incorporate a cucumber of over 20 cm in length that has a flex greater than 20 mm, in direct and enjoyable contravention of European Commission Regulation No. 1677/88.

LEGENDARY LOCAL
LUNCHES

No-nonsense nosh at noon

PIZZA Unruly Italian hotchpotch

INGREDIENTS

- Not enough beef
- Not enough cheese
- Too many anchovies

FOREIGNNESS

As foreign as
a dog on a lead
in Liverpool.

SEWAGE SAYS: **DELIVER IT BACK HOME**

This greasy mess sums up everything that is wrong with Britain today: unnecessarily complicated, full of ingredients that don't mix and what's more, there is never enough pepperoni on a Spicy Hot One. It needs to be put back in its box and sent home. Come on, Britain. It's time to take away the pizza.

THINGS TO WATCH OUT FOR

You'll probably be allocated a slice that's too small because other members round the table shout louder. Much like Brussels.

PLOUGHMAN'S Classic British mix

INGREDIENTS

- Doorsteps of bread
- Blocks of cheese
- Anything else that happens to be in or near the fridge

PREPARATION

Throw everything onto a patriotic plate. Job done.

SEWAGE SAYS:
LUNCH FOR THE LIONHEARTED

This is honest fare for hard-working British families. A brilliantly pragmatic collection of foodstuffs that doesn't fanny around with things like capers or anchovies. A big block of Cheddar, that's what you want for a meal. A ploughman's doesn't set you up for the day; it sets you up for the week.

SERVING SUGGESTION

Best eaten with friends over a pint of real ale while saying 'Parliament is sovereign' in a manner that suggests you know what that means.

HAMBURGER Haplessly hamless

INGREDIENTS

- Horse
- Meerkat
- Whatever other animal happens to wander into the slaughterhouse

FOREIGNNESS

As foreign as a man on a bike that isn't dressed like a plonker.

SEWAGE SAYS: **NO FUN IN A BUN**

For a nation as ludicrously litigious as the United States, it's odd that their only major contribution to international cuisine contravenes the Trades Descriptions Act. As anyone unfortunate enough to have eaten one knows, hamburgers don't contain ham. They also, very often, don't contain beef. They're an unappetising lawsuit in a bun.

THINGS TO WATCH OUT FOR

'Gourmet burgers' – a pathetic attempt to make eating a burger less shameful. Like calling a stripper a lapdancer.

ROAST BEEF Albion's finest

INGREDIENTS

- Beef so fresh you can still hear the echo of a moo
- Roasted potatoes and veg
- Oodles of gravy

PREPARATION

Catch it. Cook it. Carve it.

SEWAGE SAYS: THE CHURCHILL OF LUNCHES

The Sunday roast is the pivot upon which the whole week turns, the pole around which all other meals revolve. It has everything an upstanding British family needs: nutrition, tradition and gravy. The EU can straighten our bananas, they can ban smoking within five miles of a child, but they can't take away our right to overcooked meat.

SERVING SUGGESTION

Horseradish sauce adds tang to the meal, as does shaking your head in disgust at the Remoaners' attempts to subvert the WILL OF THE PEOPLE.

SUSHI A raw deal

INGREDIENTS

- Fish
- Not
- Cooked
- At
- All

FOREIGNNESS

As foreign as a vitamin in a Glaswegian's bloodstream.

SEWAGE SAYS: **ALL VERY FISHY**

Some British people claim to enjoy eating sushi but obviously they don't. They are simply trying to look cosmopolitan, to show other *Guardian* readers that they are a 'citizen of the world'. 'Look at me!', they say. 'I'm eating something that's just crawled out of the sea. How tolerant and forgiving of other cultures' stupidity am I?' A fool's errand.

THINGS TO WATCH OUT FOR

That feeling of uncertainty as to whether the cube you are forcing down is dolphin-friendly tuna or tuna-friendly dolphin.

KIPPERS No smoke without fish

INGREDIENTS

- Smoked herring
- Butter
- A pungent whiff

PREPARATION

Fry in a pan with butter until done. You know... cooked... edible. Which is what you're meant to do with food.

SEWAGE SAYS:
SMOKING HOT

APPROVED

For all self-respecting UKIPPERs, and indeed for Brexiteers in general, kippers are one of the finest British foods known to humanity. Not only do you serve them cooked, they're smoked too. Yep, that's two lots of civilisation for the price of one. Get 'em down you.

SERVING SUGGESTION

Sure, you could have them for breakfast, but why not nip home at lunchtime and smoke up a pair of beauts before returning to work and stinking out the office.

Legendary Local Lunches

TACOS Best left on the shelf

INGREDIENTS

- Taco
- Stuff placed vaguely inside the taco, ready to spill all over you

FOREIGNNESS

As foreign as a fully functioning queue in Italy.

SEWAGE SAYS: **A WACKO WAY TO EAT**

There are many challenging world records: how many fat people you can fit in a phone box; how many claustrophobics you can fit in a Mini. Now there's another one: how many spoons of chilli you can fit in a taco. The current record? Three and a half. You could feed an army on this. If your army was a seven-year-old girl.

THINGS TO WATCH OUT FOR

Eat this with a knife and fork and you'll end up with a piece of taco shell lacerating your eye.

CHEESE SARNIE Bread of heaven

SEWAGE SAYS:
BEST THING SINCE SLICED BREAD

Unlike the clam-shell structure of the taco, the sandwich is constructed using free-standing slices of bread. You can therefore fit loads of stuff in like cheese and pickle. It's filling and flexible. Basically, tacos are a laughably small shack while the sandwich is a soaring monument to greatness.

SERVING SUGGESTION

Eat during a typical British activity such as inventing the computer or being superior to the French.

CHICKEN MADRAS The spice of strife

INGREDIENTS

- Chicken
- Gunk that means you can't taste the chicken

FOREIGNNESS

As foreign as a black-and-white rainbow.

SEWAGE SAYS: **CURRY NO FAVOUR**

Chicken madras is nothing but a public health experiment served with naan. How much spice can you consume before you collapse head first into your pilau rice? This isn't food. This is come-and-have-a-go-if-you-think-you're-hard-enough.

THINGS TO WATCH OUT FOR

Turmeric. Whatever that is. The only place one should ever find turmeric is on a Scrabble board.

CHIP BUTTY The king of food

INGREDIENTS

- Chips
- Bread
- Err, that's it

PREPARATION

Make it as you would a cheese and pickle sandwich but use chips instead.

SEWAGE SAYS:
NO-NONSENSE NORTHERN NOSH

Chips. Bread. On their own they are magnificent. Together they are truly unbeatable. What's more, the chip butty is an impromptu do-it-yourself classic – just shove the chips into the bap and away you go. A cookbook could begin and end with the chip butty. As could your life.

SERVING SUGGESTION

Goes well with shouting politically incorrect abuse at a football match.

POINTLESS EU REGULATIONS TO BREAK WHILST COOKING: #3

After cooking your food, why not package and label it (even if you're just making it for yourself), ensuring that all potential allergens, e.g. arsenic and uranium-235, are missing from the label. In this way, you will pleasingly flout EU Food Information Regulation No. 1169/2011.

DOWNRIGHT
DEPENDABLE
DINNERS

For hard-working British families

SWEET-AND-SOUR PORK No ebony and ivory

INGREDIENTS

- Sweet stuff
- Sour stuff
- Pork stuff

FOREIGNNESS

As foreign as an electric guitar solo on *Songs of Praise*.

SEWAGE SAYS: **WORST OF BOTH WORLDS**

We have four distinct tastes: sweetness, sourness, saltiness and bitterness. Oh, and 'umami' – made up by the EU to create more red tape for small businesses. But here's the thing: they should all be SEPARATE. We don't put salt in our tea or lemon curd on our spuds. It's this contrary nonsense that is driving this country to the dogs. Which they also cook!

THINGS TO WATCH OUT FOR

Your dish being referred to as a number. Saying, 'I had a lovely 69 at my Chinese last night' might cause difficulties.

STEAK AND ALE PIE A great double act

INGREDIENTS

- Steak
- Ale
- Pie

PREPARATION

Bake with pride while celebrating a new multi-hundred-pound trade deal with the Falkland Islands.

SEWAGE SAYS:
ALL ALE THE PIE

The history of Britain is the triumph of simplicity over complication, of practicality over pompousness, of sturdiness over showiness. It is the triumph of steak and ale pie. What other food builds muscle and gets you over the drink-drive limit in such style?

SERVING SUGGESTION

Serve with fresh garden vegetables while reflecting on how this country invented both parliamentary democracy and darts.

SEAFOOD PAELLA Gastro-crime

INGREDIENTS

- Illegal fish
- Illegal crustaceans
- Illegal cephalopods

FOREIGNNESS

As foreign as
a driver stopping
at a pedestrian
crossing in Madrid.

SEWAGE SAYS: **THEFT ON THE HIGH SEAS**

Despite the difficulties it entails, Britain abides by the Common Fisheries Policy. Well, there doesn't seem to be much evidence of that here. Any poor creature unfortunate enough to lurk in the Mediterranean seems to be in this ludicrous Noah's Ark of a dish. Seafood paella shouldn't be eaten, it should be prosecuted.

THINGS TO WATCH OUT FOR

**65 per cent of seafood paella is unpronounceable.
85 per cent is inedible. 100 per cent is wrong.**

FISH AND CHIPS Catch of the day

INGREDIENTS

- Cod or haddock that escaped the Norwegian nets
- King Edward tats

PREPARATION

Stand to attention whilst slicing the King Edwards, then fry the fish whilst sticking two fingers up at the Norwegians.

SEWAGE SAYS:
IT'S BETTER
IN BATTER

Just like this proud island nation, fish and chips is the perfect marriage of land and sea. It's also full of saturated fat. The Nanny State and the BBC say that's bad for your health. Stuff them. If one is to die of a diet-related heart attack, it should be a heart attack made in Britain.

SERVING SUGGESTION

Wrap in yesterday's newspaper so you can be scandalised by the latest immigration figures on the way home from the chippy.

Downright Dependable Dinners

GOAT CURRY Seriously? How could you?

INGREDIENTS	FOREIGNNESS
• Freedom-loving ungulate • Spices and sauce to cover the crime	As foreign as a High Court judge in a DIY store.

SEWAGE SAYS: **THIS GETS MY GOAT**

Some animals are there to be reared, slaughtered, chopped up and cooked, while others are there to look nice. Foreign people, hear this: the proper place for a billy goat is grazing in a field, not simmering on a hob. If you're unsure, remember this rule: if you can take it to your vet, don't serve it with courgette.

THINGS TO WATCH OUT FOR

Having to say, 'Waiter, waiter! There's a goat in my curry.' No one will believe you. They'll just laugh.

SHEPHERD'S PIE
This dish isn't sheepish

INGREDIENTS

- Minced lamb
- Mashed potato
- Vegetables
- Heartiness

PREPARATION

Cover the cooked mince and veg with mash and bake whilst scoffing at experts.

SEWAGE SAYS:
NO WOOLLY THINKING HERE

If there's anything better than watching a lamb gambol in a field in our green and pleasant land then it's shoving one in an ovenproof dish and eating it. Lamb is so nutritious and tasty you'd almost think it was a vegetable. In fact, if it wasn't for the bureaucrats in Brussels, it probably would be.

SERVING SUGGESTION

Serve to guests as a hearty winter meal whilst insisting the Remoaners need to stop bleating. They lost and should just bloody well get over it.

CHILLI CON CARNE A calamity

INGREDIENTS

- Peppers
- Paprika
- Paint stripper

FOREIGNNESS

As foreign as
Vladimir Putin
caught reading
a self-help book.

SEWAGE SAYS: **CHILLI CON CARNAGE**

Alexander Fleming discovered penicillin when some mould accidentally fell into his Petri dish. It has since saved many millions of lives. The Mexicans discovered chilli con carne when the contents of a spice rack fell onto a beef dish. It has since killed millions of taste buds.

THINGS TO WATCH OUT FOR

Eating this will leave a horribly bitter taste in your mouth. Like voting Leave and still having to share a tunnel with France.

BEANS ON TOAST Beanfeast

INGREDIENTS

- Baked beans
- Buttered toast
- Magnificent simplicity

PREPARATION

Heat the beans on the hob using traditional British electricity then pour onto toast.

WORKING MAN'S WONDER

Britons eat more baked beans per capita than any other nation on earth. And that's how it should be. The only thing nobler than a baked bean is a baked bean swimming in tomato sauce atop a slice of buttered toast. But careful with that bread! The crust must not be cut off. We must protect our borders.

SERVING SUGGESTION

Best eaten whilst throwing copies of the deplorable Human Rights Act on the fire.

Downright Dependable Dinners

DONER KEBAB Pitta it won't hold together

INGREDIENTS

- Stupidly thin bread
- Meat containing DNA of no known animal

FOREIGNNESS

As foreign as a road safety campaigner with a sense of humour.

SEWAGE SAYS: **DONER DO IT**

The doner kebab is symptomatic of Europe's drastic manufacturing decline. It has dodgy raw materials, is constructed in no apparent order and falls apart quicker than a Fiat Uno left out in the rain. 'Would you like chilli sauce with that, boss?' 'No, thanks. I like my shoes the colour they are.'

THINGS TO WATCH OUT FOR

Wondering why your stomach has become an impromptu research centre for botulism.

CORNISH PASTY
This is no pastiche

INGREDIENTS

- Beef
- Potato
- Edible handles

PREPARATION

Ensure that your oven is British-made so that it is worthy of housing such a homegrown beast.

SEWAGE SAYS:
THE PRIDE OF CORNWALL

APPROVED

Foreign chefs are obsessed with concepts like 'taste' and 'flavour'. It's all about 'enjoying food'. Nonsense. The most important thing food should have is structural integrity. And that's where Cornish pasties come in. They're so solid you could build a house out of them. Or a pub. Which is another thing foreigners don't understand.

SERVING SUGGESTION

Eat outside the BMW factory in Oxford while complaining that Mini Coopers are now basically German cars.

POINTLESS EU REGULATIONS TO BREAK WHILST COOKING: #4

Once you've cooked your marvellous nosh, make a totally spurious claim for its health benefits in contravention of European Commission Regulation No. 1924/2006.

Examples include: roast beef improves your hand–eye coordination; custard can give you eternal life; pork pies help you fly.

CLEARLY COMMON-SENSE
COMESTIBLES

The snack of firm leadership

PRAWN CRACKERS Prawn fraud

INGREDIENTS

- No prawns
- Still no prawns
- Where the hell are the prawns?!

FOREIGNNESS

As foreign as a jalapeño in a Geordie's kebab.

SEWAGE SAYS: **YOU MUST BE CRACKERS**

First question: where's the prawn? Nowhere, that's where. These crackers are basically homeopathic food. No prawn, just the memory of prawn. If you left some styrofoam overnight on Brighton Pier, you'd create a finer seafood snack than this. File under 'total and utter disgrace'.

THINGS TO WATCH OUT FOR

Having to eat these on a drip to prevent salt-induced dehydration.

PORK SCRATCHINGS Superlative snack

INGREDIENTS

- Not sure, to be honest, but there is probably a pig's eyebrow in there somewhere

---

PREPARATION

Can only be bought in pubs with fruit machines and wall-to-wall carpets.

SEWAGE SAYS:
PUTS HAIRS ON YOUR CHEST

In this age of obsessive, neo-narcissistic health concerns, pork scratchings have become the pariahs of pub snacks. Eat these and you'll be accused of attempted suicide. But pork scratchings have helped make Britain what it is today. A country full of people who should live a lot longer than we do.

SERVING SUGGESTION

To be washed down with a port and brandy while arguing that British police officers should not be able to speak a foreign language.

Clearly Common-Sense Comestibles

POPPADOMS Oversized crisps

INGREDIENTS	FOREIGNNESS
• Oversized flour • Oversized vegetable oil	As foreign as a Media Studies graduate building something useful like a bridge.

SEWAGE SAYS: **POP THEM ON A PLANE**

Poppadoms are, let's face it, big crisps. And crisps should come ready-broken in packets. Having to break them up yourself is just a load of bureaucratic nonsense. And then they expect you to dip them in things! Ridiculous! The poppadom must learn its true place in the hierarchy of wafer-thin fried carbohydrates. At the bottom of the pile.

THINGS TO WATCH OUT FOR

You'd assume they come in different flavours like proper crisps. But no. Nothing. Not even cheese and onion. Just bland nonsense. Appalling.

CRISPS Proper-sized crisps

INGREDIENTS

- Potatoes
- Oil
- Salt
- FLAVOURS!

PREPARATION

Don't bother.
Available from all
good crisp outlets.

SEWAGE SAYS:
CRISPY GOODNESS

Practical and character-building, the humble potato crisp is at the heart of our national life. Imagine a childhood without licking the salt and vinegar flavour off your fingers. Impossible. So, go on. Give your child the gift of cherished memories. Give them salt-induced hypertension. Give them crisps.

SERVING SUGGESTION

Best eaten in the pub accompanying a decent British ale while discussing how the EU put the FFS into trade tariffs.

OLIVES Why would you bother?

INGREDIENTS	FOREIGNNESS
• Fruit of the olive tree grown to provide shade for lazy farmers	As foreign as a Russian athlete's blood in a Russian athlete.

SEWAGE SAYS: **A POOR MAN'S PLUM**

VETOED

If anything can explain why the European Union is doomed, it's the olive. Guests are offered a bowl of them and invited to take a couple. But they're so small everyone keeps coming back for more, dipping their fingers into the magic communal bowl. Until, of course, the olives run out and everyone blames the Germans.

THINGS TO WATCH OUT FOR

Like the voice of a BBC continuity announcer, the olive is only the prelude to something even more disappointing.

STUFF ON A STICK You won't feel a prick

INGREDIENTS

- Cheese and pineapple
- Pickled onions
- Mini sausages
- Basically, anything that will go on a stick!

PREPARATION

Put the stuff on sticks. Sorted.

SEWAGE SAYS:
HIT ON A STICK

APPROVED

You know what you're getting with cheese and pineapple on a stick. You're getting cheese and pineapple on a stick. Same goes for your pickled onion and your cocktail sausage. Basically, you get out what you put in. Which is more than can be said of the EU membership fee.

SERVING SUGGESTION

With cheese, attach a little Union Jack to each stick to make it absolutely clear this is common-sense British fare – none of this pretentious 'runny' foreign nonsense.

MAYONNAISE French fancy

INGREDIENTS

- White gloop
- White gunk
- Vinegar

FOREIGNNESS

As foreign as bead curtains in a nuclear fallout shelter.

SEWAGE SAYS: **PROMISCUITY IN A JAR**

It is no accident that the moral decline of Britain has coincided with the rise of mayonnaise. A dressing should pair itself with a dish and live monogamously ever after. Not mayonnaise. It flaunts itself as a dressing for all occasions. 'Come here,' she whispers, 'and I shall spread myself for you – anytime, anywhere, on anything.' Beware this floozy!

THINGS TO WATCH OUT FOR

Eating it and expecting to enjoy it, particularly once a splodge of the damned stuff has dripped down your front and into your lap.

GRAVY The lifeblood of Britain

INGREDIENTS

- Beef stock
- Okay, chicken or lamb stock if you must
- Definitely not vegetable or onion stock

PREPARATION

Pour hot water on the stock and stir.

SEWAGE SAYS:
A SAUCE OF HOPE

Gravy is a fine and faithful sauce. It's poured on meat, veg and potatoes and that's it. When you reach for that stock cube, you know what to expect of gravy and gravy knows what to expect of you. Make it as thick as an EU directive or as thin as a Remainer's excuses. The choice is yours.

SERVING SUGGESTION

Ladle onto roast beef and Yorkshire pudding as a tear of patriotic pride rolls down your cheek.

Clearly Common-Sense Comestibles

HUMMUS A heap of halitosis

INGREDIENTS	FOREIGNNESS
• Suspicious beige stuff • Little bits of who-knows-what	As foreign as a chastity belt in Magaluf.

SEWAGE SAYS: **SHORT FOR HURLSOME MUSH**

If the spirit of the EU could be rendered in food, it would be hummus. Ingredients that can get on perfectly well on their own, together become a useless splodge of blandness. If the chickpea can be liberated from this homogeneous mush then so can we.

THINGS TO WATCH OUT FOR

Friends assuming that you are seriously ill as you don't appear to be eating solids.

HP SAUCE Ooh, you are saucy

SEWAGE SAYS: ONCE YOU'VE HAD BROWN...

APPROVED

This spicy delight isn't a condiment, it's a genuine snack. Eat it with chips and you know the chip is simply a brown sauce delivery system. If you had to take three items with you on a desert island, it should be a Boris Johnson calendar, a Union Jack and a bottle of HP.

SERVING SUGGESTION

Can be eaten on its own but also goes well with other British food such as chips, chip butties and overcooked roast beef.

GUACAMOLE Unholy moly

INGREDIENTS

- Lime
- Chilli
- Avocado
- Stuff that shouldn't get past customs

FOREIGNNESS

As foreign as a Marxist at the Last Night of the Proms.

SEWAGE SAYS: **GREEN, UNPLEASANT, BLAND**

These days, the fashion for trying new things has got completely out of hand. Why else would anyone want to eat this Day-Glo muck? We must stick to what we know and what we know works best. In Britain, avocado is, and will always be, the colour of your bathroom suite.

THINGS TO WATCH OUT FOR

The Aztecs ate this stuff. Do you want to eat the food of a failed civilisation?

MUSHY PEAS
Peas peas me

INGREDIENTS

- Lots of sugar
- Lots of salt
- Add peas to taste

PREPARATION

Soak the peas overnight with baking soda while you get soaked with gin.

SEWAGE SAYS:
GIVE PEAS A CHANCE

Okra, yam, cassava, papaya. No, they're not recent winners of the Prize for Overseas Fiction, they're fruit and veg that might end up on your plate in happy-clappy liberal London. It's political correctness gone bonkers. What this country needs is British veg for hard-working British people. What this country needs is peas. Mushed up a bit. Mushy peas.

SERVING SUGGESTION

Eat with chunky chips in the depths of winter while wearing a northern football shirt. Like fans of Newcastle Utd. Or that other northern city.

Clearly Common-Sense Comestibles

TARAMASALATA Pink slime

INGREDIENTS

- Lemon juice and milk!
- Olive oil and fish eggs!
- No, really!

FOREIGNNESS

As foreign as a
condom machine
in a convent.

SEWAGE SAYS: **DON'T DIP INTO THIS**

Is there anything more hilarious than a dip made from fish eggs? Yes, at some point in history some foreigner saw a fresh cod and thought, 'Hey. We can remove the roe, mix it with lemon juice, milk and olive oil and call it food.' You can't make this stuff up. We gave the world the Industrial Revolution. They gave us indigestion.

THINGS TO WATCH OUT FOR

Whatever you do, for God's sake don't let your kids mistake it for Angel Delight. The poor sods will have nightmares for a week.

SCOTCH EGG Hard-boiled hero

INGREDIENTS

- Egg
- The outside stuff that goes round the egg

PREPARATION

Cover the egg in the outside stuff until it's perfectly spherical. Marvel at the roundness of it all.

SEWAGE SAYS:
AS SURE AS EGGS IS EGGS

When a chicken lays an egg it has two devout wishes. First, that it grows up to be a proud British chicken like its mother. Second, that it becomes a Scotch egg. No other country could produce this snack. No other country could eat this snack. No other country would even consider this snack. Be proud.

SERVING SUGGESTION

Purchase from a poorly refrigerated unit in a motorway service station, then eat while driving at 77 mph singing along to *Great Driving Power Ballads Volume IV*.

HOW TO MAINTAIN
A HARD BREXIT: #1

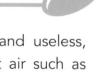

To avoid your Brexit going soft and useless, keep it away from sources of hot air such as Supreme Court judges, Keir Starmer or any Liberal Democrat.

If this cannot be avoided, using the following words and phrases will ensure your Brexit regains its proper unyielding consistency: the will of the people; 52:48; we won, you lost; suck it up, losers.

STAUNCHLY SIMPLE
STARTERS

Not a Maastricht morsel in sight

BORSCHT Disgrace from behind the Iron Curtain

INGREDIENTS

- Probably some sort of ritual animal blood
- Radioactive water from Chernobyl

FOREIGNNESS

As foreign as eating outdoors.

SEWAGE SAYS: **SIMPLY THE WORSCHT**

This beetroot-based soup is popular in Ukraine, Belarus, Poland, Estonia, Lithuania, Latvia, blah, blah, blah. If it was entered into the Eurovision Song Contest it would win by a mile. And what would an unpretentious British soup get? That's right. *Nul points.* Borscht is a liquid symbol of all that is wrong with Europe. It's time to fight back. It's time to slurp British!

THINGS TO WATCH OUT FOR

If you spill some, it'll leave a horrible red stain – just like the Warsaw Pact. And it'll take just as long to wash away.

BEETROOT SOUP
Delight from this sceptred isle

INGREDIENTS

- British beetroot
- British water
- British salt
- British pepper

PREPARATION

Bring to the boil whilst humming 'Jerusalem'.

SEWAGE SAYS:
IMPOSSIBLE TO BEET

When they start serving borscht at your local golf club you know you're in trouble. It is unbridled immigration in a bowl. Ensure the integrity of our nation's borders by insisting upon good, solid, hearty British beetroot soup instead. How to tell if you're supping on beetroot soup and not some foreign muck? Ask yourself, 'Are you in Britain?' If 'yes', then yes. Sorted.

SERVING SUGGESTION

Best enjoyed while bemoaning the number of bilingual people in Britain.

PICKLED HERRING A bit of a pickle

INGREDIENTS

- Socialist fish
- Left-wing vinegar

FOREIGNNESS

As foreign as an amusing politically correct comedian.

SEWAGE SAYS: **FEED IT TO THE CAT**

With their generous benefits, good childcare and love of the environment, you might think Scandinavia is a socialist utopia. That's until you look at what they have to eat: pickled fish. That's right, folks – they've spent so much money on biodegradable ABBA CDs and carbon-neutral vibrators they can't afford to cook their own food.

THINGS TO WATCH OUT FOR

Every time you eat this stuff, you're just encouraging social democracy.

JELLIED EELS East End elegance

INGREDIENTS

- Eels
- Some sort of jelly to put the eels in

PREPARATION

Kill the eel, chop it up, boil it, allow it to cool. Sorted, guv'nor.

SEWAGE SAYS:
THE REEL DEEL

We British are excellent at putting food in jars: strawberry jam, raspberry jam and jellied eels. Name something of worth that foreigners have put in a jar? Einstein's brain. Yeah. Try eating that. Jellied eels don't seem so bad now, do they?

SERVING SUGGESTION

Best enjoyed while flouting the EU Working Time Directive.

Staunchly Simple Starters

BRUSCHETTA Random stuff on bread

INGREDIENTS

- Stuff from the back of the cupboard
- Stuff stuck to the back of the fridge

FOREIGNNESS

As foreign as a poetry reading in a motorway service station.

SEWAGE SAYS: **WILL MAKE YOU BRUSQUE**

Onion, tomato, basil, balsamic vinegar, olive oil. No, that's not the contents of a salad, it's what the Italians think is acceptable to put on bread. If you can call bruschetta bread. Honestly. You'd have to be high on illegal drugs to come up with such a ludicrous concoction and you'd have to be even higher on even more illegal drugs to eat it.

THINGS TO WATCH OUT FOR

Whatever you do, for heaven's sake don't pronounce it correctly. Do you want to be mistaken for a Liberal Democrat MEP?

BREAD AND DRIPPING

Fat on toast.
And why not.

INGREDIENTS

- Animal fat
- Bread
- A knife and a plate to reassure you that it is food

PREPARATION

Place a slab of fat on the bread. Eat it. Enjoy it.

SEWAGE SAYS:
MAY THE LARD SAVE US

They say coal and iron was the fuel of the Industrial Revolution. Poppycock. It was bread and dripping. Generations of northerners not only survived on this stuff, they ate it for fun. Vitamins, fibre, antioxidants. You won't find any of that nonsense here. Bread and dripping is for men.

SERVING SUGGESTION

Turn the lights off, crouch under the kitchen table and imagine you're eating it down a coal mine.

SAUERKRAUT Sour shredded cabbage – ugh

INGREDIENTS

- Shredded cabbage
- Lactic acid and bacteria. That's right. Bacteria. On purpose.

FOREIGNNESS

As foreign as a trampoline in an old people's home.

SEWAGE SAYS: **NEIN, FRITZ!**

Let's be clear. Pickled cabbage must not get a foothold in our national diet. Before we know it, we will be ending our sentences with verbs and developing a highly efficient value-added manufacturing sector. That's just not British. We will fight it in Tesco; we will fight it in Waitrose; to sour cabbage, we will never surrender.

THINGS TO WATCH OUT FOR

Jars of this outrage are taking up valuable shelf space that could be devoted to more patriotic foods like jellied eels and Marmite.

CABBAGE SOUP
Cabbage broth. Yum.

INGREDIENTS

- Cabbage, water, salt and pepper. You'd think there'd be more to it, but you'd be very much mistaken.

PREPARATION

Boil the cabbage in the water until it becomes soup-like.

SEWAGE SAYS:
CABBAGE WITHOUT THE BAGGAGE

APPROVED

Nothing says 'Britain' better than good old cabbage soup. It's a classic hot meal, it's devastatingly nutritious and if you hold your nose while you eat it, you'll even think it tastes good. Brilliant for curing colds and lowering culinary expectations.

SERVING SUGGESTION

Best eaten sitting at the dinner table while discussing how the euro is simply a new form of German imperialism.

Staunchly Simple Starters

GARLIC BREAD For vampire hunters only

INGREDIENTS

- Self-regarding bread
- Smug garlic

FOREIGNNESS

As foreign as a human rights lawyer that you don't want to punch in the face.

SEWAGE SAYS: **A STINKER**

You might think this is a harmless snack or starter, but if you do, you'd be dead wrong. Garlic bread is an outrider of EU totalitarianism. If we continue to accept this as part of our national diet, they know we will accept anything. First garlic bread, then electric cars, and before you know it, Angela Bloody Merkel telling you how to wipe your backside.

THINGS TO WATCH OUT FOR

Restaurants trying to dupe you into thinking this is acceptable as a starter.

MARMITE ON TOAST Toasty

INGREDIENTS

- Sovereign bread
- Independent butter
- Free Marmite

PREPARATION

Spread the Marmite on the toast with a stainless knife forged in the steelworks of Sheffield.

SEWAGE SAYS:
A FEAST OF YEAST

Yeast is responsible for three of the greatest things known to mankind: beer, bread and Marmite. You could live on nothing else for a month and still be able to swim the English Channel in your Union Jack underpants. Yeast might be a eukaryotic microorganism but there's no EU about it at all. This fine, freedom-loving fungus is British through and through.

SERVING SUGGESTION

Throw the toast in the air. It will land Marmite-side up. Unlike top-heavy state-subsidised foreign toast.

HOW TO MAINTAIN
A HARD BREXIT: #2

All ingredients such as free movement and single market access should be avoided. They will only dilute your Brexit, causing it to lose its robustness and strength. If you feel your Brexit softening, stiffen your resolve by beating yourself about the face with a copy of the *Daily Express* while singing 'Rule Britannia'.

MAJESTIC
MONOCULTURAL
MAINS

No offshore offal on offer here

WIENER SCHNITZEL Austrian abomination

INGREDIENTS

- Lifeless calf
- Pointless breadcrumbs
- Silly name

FOREIGNNESS

As foreign as a tomato in a fruit salad.

SEWAGE SAYS: **YOU DIED IN VAIN, YOUNG CALF**

It's hard to write about Wiener schnitzel without contravening the UK Race Relations Act 1976. Meat in breadcrumbs? That's not just wrong, it's immoral. Thankfully this frightful dish has yet to become as established in the national diet as other invasive species. We cannot rest on our laurels, though. These Teutons do have ways of making us eat.

THINGS TO WATCH OUT FOR

When the chef's 'recommendation' becomes the chef saying, 'You will have this or else,' you know it's going to be Wiener schnitzel.

VEAL PIE British pre-beef beauty

INGREDIENTS

- Meat of a young calf (best not to think about it)
- Pastry

PREPARATION

Place the veal in the pastry and cook in an oven until it becomes a pie.

SEWAGE SAYS:
PROPER DISH FOR PROPER CATTLE

There is surely nothing more British than a pie. Solid and dependable. Filling, not flashy. Forget free education or high-speed broadband, every British child should have unfettered access to overcooked, inhumanely reared animal in pastry. It's the bedrock of our proud island nation.

SERVING SUGGESTION

Eat while cultivating a dashed fine moustache and watching reruns of _The Dam Busters_.

Majestic Monocultural Mains

GOULASH Flash name for plain food

INGREDIENTS

- Foreign steak
- Foreign onions
- Paprika
  (all paprika is foreign)

FOREIGNNESS

As foreign as a Viking at a peace conference.

SEWAGE SAYS: **I'D RATHER GO HUNGARY**

Goulash is basically stew. But because it's got a fancy-sounding foreign name, the metropolitan liberal elite think it's superior to our own meat-based casseroles. You don't travel to work on a *vonat*, do you? Or sit on a *szék*? No. Because they're Hungarian words and this isn't Hungary. Yet. So, come on. Let's reassert ourselves. Let's call a spade a spade. Let's call a stew a stew.

THINGS TO WATCH OUT FOR

Ask for something that starts with 'gou' and you WILL get goo.

STEW Meat. Potatoes. Bosh.

INGREDIENTS

- Potatoes
- Meat
- Carrots
- Simplicity

PREPARATION

Chop it all up and shove it in the oven before going for a frame of snooker.

SEWAGE SAYS:
STEW-PENDOUS

The unapologetically British word 'stew' is both a noun and a verb: you can eat stew and you can stew meat. Not that anyone under the age of 50 would know the bleeding difference. New-fangled lefty teaching methods must be dropped in favour of teaching kids grammar. Ideally with the threat of low-level violence. Ideally after a plate of stew.

SERVING SUGGESTION

To be savoured while believing everything you see written on the side of a big red bus.

MOULES MARINIÈRE Never mind the molluscs

INGREDIENTS

- Moules – that's mussels to you and me
- Marinières – nope, not a clue

FOREIGNNESS

As foreign as a cyclist waiting patiently at a red traffic light.

SEWAGE SAYS: **COMPLETE FAFF**

If you've never had mussels in white wine and garlic, count yourself lucky. It's a 90:10 meal. Ninety per cent of the time is spent trying to eat the last ten per cent of it. Just when you think you've found the last mussel, another appears from under some now completely stone-cold fries. A plate is where a meal should take place, not the venue for a game of mollusc hide and seek.

THINGS TO WATCH OUT FOR

Expending more calories hunting down and opening the shells than you gain from eating their meagre garlic-soaked contents.

FISH FINGERS Nothing fishy about these

INGREDIENTS

- Fish in a finger
- Breadcrumbs

PREPARATION

Buy from any self-respecting supermarket. If they don't stock them, write to your MP or engage in civil disobedience.

SEWAGE SAYS:
A BIG THUMBS UP

Fish may taste great but they are a ludicrous shape. All that tail and fins business means you can't fit one in a lunchbox or a sandwich. It took a British genius to recognise this, and so the magnificent fish finger was born. It is an ode to order, a paean to pragmatism. It is brilliance in breadcrumbs.

SERVING SUGGESTION

Align the fingers perpendicularly to the edge of the table in front of you. This is not a suggestion. Anything else would be disrespectful to the spirit of the fish finger.

CHOW MEIN

Chow down at your peril

INGREDIENTS

- Noodles
- Chicken, perhaps
- Soy sauce, if you must

FOREIGNNESS

As foreign as dwarf-throwing at the *Guardian* office party.

SEWAGE SAYS: **SAY NO TO NOODLES**

People have been eating noodles for over 4,000 years. Which is not surprising because it's almost impossible to wrap them round your fork. And don't even think about using chopsticks. It's like trying to pick up a fresh turd with a piece of string.

THINGS TO WATCH OUT FOR

Finishing your meal then immediately wanting never to eat such a thing again.

CHICKEN PIE

It's chicken in a pie

INGREDIENTS

- Chicken
  (free range, if you feel the need)
- Pastry

PREPARATION

Cook the same as veal pie, substituting chicken for the veal. The pie bit stays the same.

SEWAGE SAYS:
THIS CHICKEN'S GOT WINGS

Chicken pie is a national treasure, the Clare Balding of meat-filled baked pastry. It is food for the people, of the people, by the people. It is not chicken en croute or chicken à la pie. It is, gloriously, unaffectedly... a pie... with chicken in it.

SERVING SUGGESTION

Eat while bemoaning the number of people who are descended from foreigners on *Who Do You Think You Are?*

Majestic Monocultural Mains

HOW TO MAINTAIN
A HARD BREXIT: #3

So-called 'experts' such as law professors, judges, diplomats, trade negotiators and economic historians might try to soften up your Brexit. It is therefore imperative to keep it in a Brexit-friendly environment. Such places include your local golf club, every retirement home or any coastal resort with a Butlin's.

PROPERLY PATRIOTIC
PUDDINGS

EU'll get your just desserts

CRÈME BRÛLÉE French farce

INGREDIENTS

- Cream (burned)
- Sugar (burned)

FOREIGNNESS

As foreign as a vegetarian in an all-you-can-eat zoo.

SEWAGE SAYS: **A CRIME AGAINST COOKING**

Let us unmask this fancy Dan of a dessert for what it really is: a splodge of burned cream. No, sorry. Sometimes there's some burned sugar on top too. Yes, the French have elevated their inability to cook into a national dish. Not only that, but crème brûlée contravenes the great rule of British dining: never ever eat anything that contains an accent.

THINGS TO WATCH OUT FOR

A dish so small that neither your spoon nor your tongue will fit inside it. You look at it helplessly for a moment before taking it home and feeding it to your dog.

CUSTARD A just dessert

INGREDIENTS

- The sap of the custard tree
- Vanilla flavouring

PREPARATION

Whisk, then put in a saucepan and cook on a low heat while marvelling at the yellowness of it all.

APPROVED

Custard is the foot soldier of the sweet course. Unglamorous but gets the job done. You can eat it on its own, pour it on something or hide things in it. It is neither liquid nor solid, neither too sweet nor too bland – a quivering, luscious lump of magnificent British ingenuity.

SERVING SUGGESTION

Can be eaten on its own or with people who share your penchant for hard Brexit.

TIRAMISU An utter mess

INGREDIENTS

- Coffee (seriously)
- Wine (no, really)
- Cream (we think)

FOREIGNNESS

As foreign as a complimentary glass of champagne on a Ryanair flight.

SEWAGE SAYS: **WE WON'T MISS YOU**

Along with oversized pepper grinders and over-familiar staff, every restaurant seems to be blighted by this ghastly offering. Just take a look at the ingredients – espresso and wine! Can you believe it? The only time your dessert should contain coffee and wine is when you've had a bloody good evening and knocked your drinks over.

THINGS TO WATCH OUT FOR

Suddenly having the urge to wear your sunglasses at night and shout 'ciao bella' while driving a moped really badly.

SPOTTED DICK Down-to-earth pudding

INGREDIENTS

- Suet, flour, raisins, cinnamon and stuff like that

PREPARATION

Mix ingredients and steam for 90 minutes while constantly sniggering to yourself.

A proper dessert with straight-down-the-line ingredients like sponge and currants. What's more, it upholds the great British tradition of harmless sexual innuendo, giving pleasure to customers in restaurants everywhere: 'How large will my Spotted Dick be?' and 'I'm going to place my Spotted Dick on the table and take a photo.' Quality.

SERVING SUGGESTION

Best eaten while watching one of the greatest films ever made: *Carry On Dick*.

Properly Patriotic Puddings

PAVLOVA What a palaver

INGREDIENTS

- Caster sugar
- Cornflour
- Don't bother. It gets worse.

FOREIGNNESS

As foreign as a skiing instructor who doesn't try to seduce your wife.

SEWAGE SAYS: LIKE EATING A FROZEN TEA COSY

Pavlova is proof that you can create evil from anything, even meringue and fruit. Just look at it. It manages to be pompous, vain and inedible all at the same time. Pavlova was apparently created in honour of a Russian dancer touring the antipodes in the 1920s. What the hell did she do? Defecate on the Australian flag?

THINGS TO WATCH OUT FOR

Suffering ten years' worth of tooth decay in five minutes.

SEMOLINA Proper school dessert

INGREDIENTS

- Semolina and milk
- Maybe a splodge of jam

PREPARATION

Mix the semolina and milk together until it looks like watery porridge.

SEWAGE SAYS:
WILL SCAR YOU – IN A GOOD WAY

Other nations consider desserts to be fun, frivolous or even something to look forward to. Not so in Britain. We think a dessert should be character-building. When it's placed in front of you, you feel fear and respect. Life isn't a bowl of cherries; life is a bowl of congealed semolina pudding.

SERVING SUGGESTION

Best given to a young child while telling them the European Single Market will rob them of their future and that Father Christmas doesn't exist.

HOW TO MAINTAIN
A HARD BREXIT: #4

There has been much discussion about the varying degrees of hardness and softness of Brexit as though it were a toilet roll. Brexit is not a toilet roll. As we know, Brexit means Brexit. And a red, white and blue Brexit means a red, white and blue Brexit. And, naturally, a hard red, white and blue Brexit means a hard red, white and blue Brexit. So, we hope that clears things up.

BULLISHLY BRITISH
BEVERAGES

Liquid gumption in a glass

WINE Fruit juice ruined

INGREDIENTS

- Mouldy grape skin
- Foot sweat

FOREIGNNESS

As foreign as a leaflet shoved through your door that you actually want to read.

SEWAGE SAYS: **A WASTE OF GRAPES**

Is there anything more un-British than a wine-drinker? Just listen to the tripe they come out with: 'I'm getting a hint of cinnamon here, a flirtation of pomegranate, a come-hither wink of something or other.' Balderdash. I'll tell you what you get if you drink wine: the sneer of an expensively subsidised ungrateful peasant.

THINGS TO WATCH OUT FOR

Mistaking the wine list for a ransom note.

GIN AND TONIC What a tonic

INGREDIENTS

- Gin
- Tonic
- Ice
- Lemon
- Class

PREPARATION

Throw your wife the car keys and pour yourself a large one.

SEWAGE SAYS:
TG FOR G&T

This was the preferred tipple of the men who ran the Empire. The tonic protected against malaria and the gin protected against sobriety. And it's still a winning combination of health and happiness today. The Queen Mother drank it on her 100th birthday as she asked her daughter, 'Where's my bloody telegram, then?' God rest her soul and God bless gin and tonic.

SERVING SUGGESTION

Sup on this while explaining that Article 50 was written by a Brit so it can mean anything we bloody well want.

LATTE Scourge of the high street

INGREDIENTS

- Far too much milk
- Some coffee, so they claim
- Nothing that warrants the price

FOREIGNNESS

As foreign as
a snooker table
in a caravan.

SEWAGE SAYS: **A GLASS OF HOT MILK RUINED**

Skinny latte, soy latte, frappe latte, vanilla latte: there are more varieties than there are ways to enter Britain illegally. It is modern life gone frothing mad. Not only that, it requires a ludicrously complex machine to make it – usually operated by someone doing 'training'. You want a drink, not an insight into how crap someone can be on their first day at work.

THINGS TO WATCH OUT FOR

Comes in a top-heavy glass that teeters on its tiny saucer, accompanied by a stupidly long spoon that serves no purpose other than to poke you in the eye when drinking.

TEA A pukka cuppa

INGREDIENTS

- Tea leaves
- Hot water
- Milk and sugar

PREPARATION

Being able to make a decent brew is a standard test of mental competence. By that criterion, the rest of the world is barking mad.

SEWAGE SAYS:
THE KING OF HOT DRINKS

Like democracy, we might not have invented it but, by God, have we made it our own. Just take the noble British brickie. His veins don't run with blood, they run with 'milk and five sugars'. Take tea and Page 3 away from him, and he's practically Eastern European. Basically, if you don't test positive for tea then you're not one of us.

SERVING SUGGESTION

English breakfast tea is like a traditional English breakfast, so damned fine that you can have it at any time of the day.

Bullishly British Beverages

LAGER Produces continental hangovers

INGREDIENTS

- Bottom-fermenting yeast
- Too much fizz
- Not enough class

FOREIGNNESS

As foreign as a drum 'n' bass DJ at a funeral.

SEWAGE SAYS: **URINAL TAP**

Lager is a comically bland substance made by faceless 'beerocrats' in Europe. During the production process any semblance of taste and originality is identified, then carefully removed. Just like they do with their goddam awful so-called 'pop' music.

THINGS TO WATCH OUT FOR

Consoling yourself with the thought that your hangover was reassuringly expensive.

REAL ALE The real deal

INGREDIENTS

- Top-fermenting yeast
- Malted barley and hops

PREPARATION

Go to your local and if they can't offer a pint of Old Fudger's Cockstrap, call the police.

SEWAGE SAYS:
A PINT WELL MADE

When Britain ruled the world, a worker would drink pints of ale at lunch before going back to the factory. The result? The Jaguar E-type and Concorde. We built them with smiles on our faces. Because we were pissed. Forget what the Nanny State tells you: you must drink this stuff before operating heavy machinery.

SERVING SUGGESTION

Quaff in a thatched inn by a village green as you reflect on the fact that a pint is vastly superior to 0.568 litres.

ACKNOWLEDGEMENTS

We give hearty thanks to:

Aaron Budhram, Adam Morley, Alan Dow, Alan Fox, Alex Fife, Alex Phillips, Angela Fox, Bake Me, Chris Orrow, Daniel Gosling, David Laurence, Debbie Sawyer, Dominique Harris, Elżbieta Marach-Dunajko, Emily Green, Field's, Fiona Underhill, Gareth Warmingham, Helen Orton, James Worger, Jane Pepe, John Gowers, Katie Duncombe, Leon Mayo, libdemvoice.org, Louisa Gummer, Mary Reid, Miranda Thomas, Patrick Xavier Green, Paul Sawyer, Reiko Oishi Laurence, Ric Wegener, Seán Harte, Simon Barker, Stephen Pepper, Steve Kirkpatrick, Sylvia Odolant, Tom Pride, UKIP Weather and Yvonne Mowberry.

MORE ACKNOWLEDGEMENTS

And especially hearty thanks to:

Abbie Headon, Adam Poplawski, Claire Blake-Will, Claire Plimmer, Debbie Chapman, Edwina Blake-Will, Emma Taylor, Ewa Blake-Will, Julia Mills, Julie Harris, Marcella Toth, Michelle Kirkpatrick, Mick and Boo Dwyer, Paul Bowers, Patrick Green, Robert Wegenek, Rod and Pat Bower and Tanya Tier.

With extra special patriotic thanks to:

The hard-working families of Britain without whom this great country would not have been possible.

Marc Blakewill & James Harris
www.blakewillandharris.com

Have you enjoyed this book?
If so, why not write a review on your favourite website?

If you're interested in finding out more about our books, find
us on Facebook at **Summersdale Publishers** and follow us
on Twitter at **@Summersdale**.

Thanks very much for buying this Summersdale book.

www.summersdale.com